Counting Books

Snowflakes and Ice Skates

A Winter Counting Book

by Rebecca Fjelland Davis

Reading Consultant: Jennifer Norford
Senior Consultant: Mid-continent for Research and Education

Capstone
Mankato, MN

A+ books TM

A+ Books are published by Capstone Press,
151 Good Counsel Drive, P.O. Box 669, Mankato, Minnesota 56002.
www.capstonepress.com

Printed in the United States of America

1 2 3 4 5 6 11 10 09 08 07 06

Library of Congress Cataloging-in-Publication Data

Davis, Rebecca Fjelland.
Snowflakes and ice skates : a winter counting book / by Rebecca Fjelland
Davis.
p. cm.—(A+ books. Counting books)
Includes bibliographical references and index.
ISBN-13: 978-0-7368-5379-8 (hardcover)
ISBN-10: 0-7368-5379-0 (hardcover)
1. Counting—Juvenile literature. 2. Winter—Juvenile literature. I.
Title. II. Series.
QA113.D388 2006
513.2'11—dc22
2005019061

Credits

Jenny Marks, editor; Ted Williams, designer; Karon Dubke, photographer; Kelly Garvin,
photo researcher

Photo Credits

Capstone Press, Karon Dubke, cover, 2–3 (all), 8–9, 10–11, 12–13, 16–17(all), 18–19 (all), 22–23 (all),
26 (all), 27 (mittens), 28, 29
Corbis/Richard Cummins, 20–21, 27 (icicles); Tom Stewart, 24–25
Getty Images/The Imagebank/Per Eriksson, 14–15
Masterfile/Andrew Wenzel, 6–7
Superstock/James Urbach, 5

Note to Parents, Teachers, and Librarians

Snowflakes and Ice Skates uses color photographs and a rhyming nonfiction format to introduce
children to various signs of the winter season while building mastery of basic counting skills. It is
designed to be read aloud to a pre-reader or to be read independently by an early reader. The images
help early readers and listeners understand the text and concepts discussed. The book encourages
further learning by the following sections: Facts about Winter, Words to Know, Read More, Internet
Sites, and Index. Early readers may need assistance using these features.

In the winter season trees are bare.
Cold winds blow most everywhere.
But skating and sledding are so much fun.
Let's count winter things one by one.

One red cardinal sings
in the tree. Even in the cold,
he's happy as can be.

2

Two smiling snowmen
stand side by side.
The weather is freezing,
but they won't come inside.

Three pine trees grow
so straight and tall.
They are forever green,
so their needles don't fall.

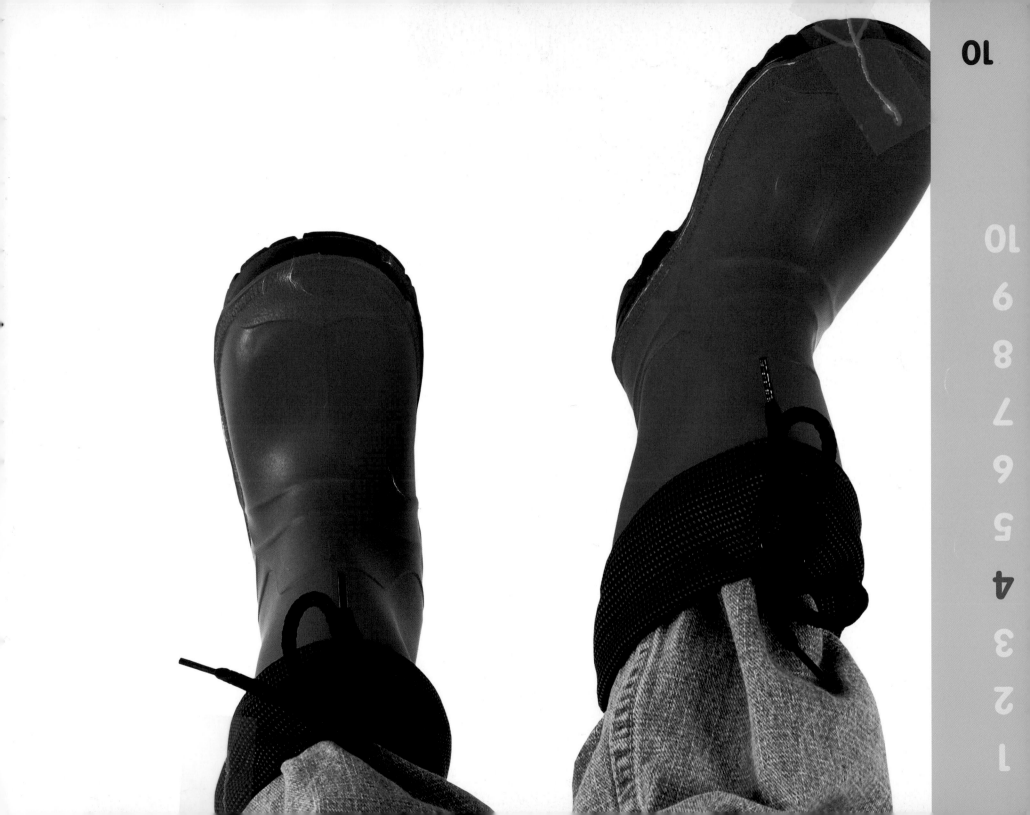

Four red snow boots,
let's give them a try.
They'll keep your toes
cozy, warm, and dry.

4

1 2 3 4 5 6 7 8 9 10

Five eager skaters have fun
on the ice. Oops! When you fall,
it doesn't feel so nice.

Six sled dogs hear the shout of "MUSH!" That's their signal to take off in a rush.

Seven bright sleds, ready
for the snow. Slide down
the hill, come on, let's go!

7

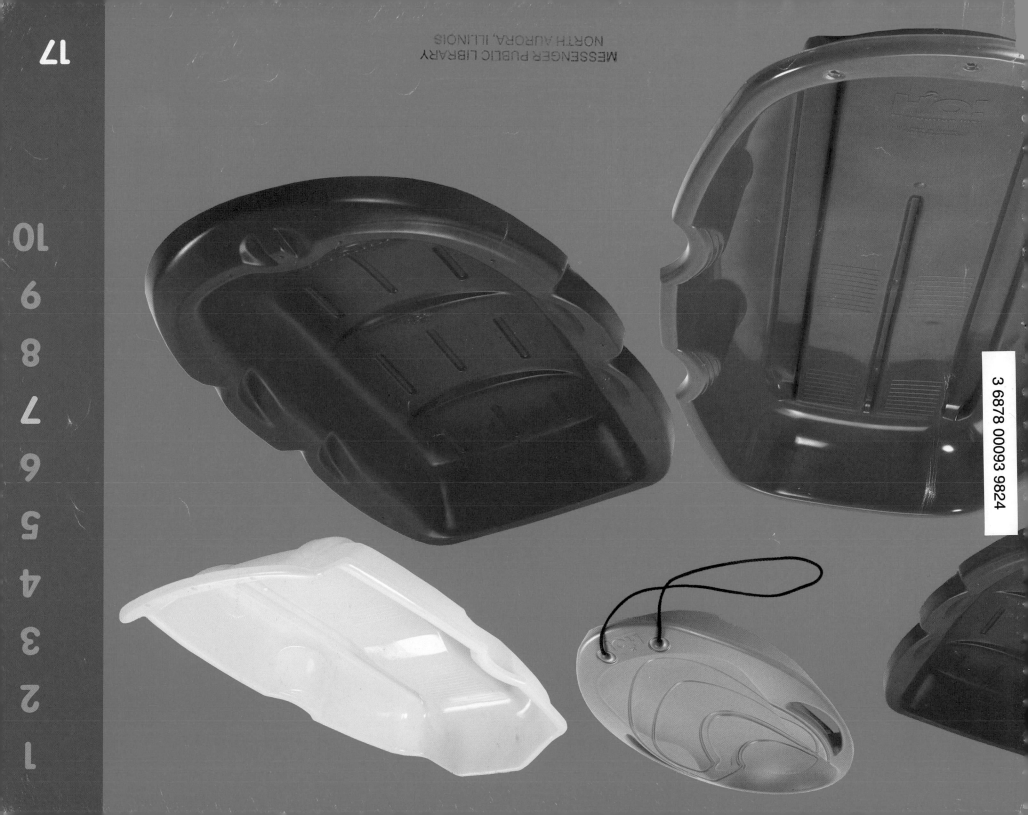

Eight warm mittens
are for hands to wear.
Thumbs stand alone
but fingers must share.

Nine shiny icicles hang
in a row. Should one drop,
watch out below!

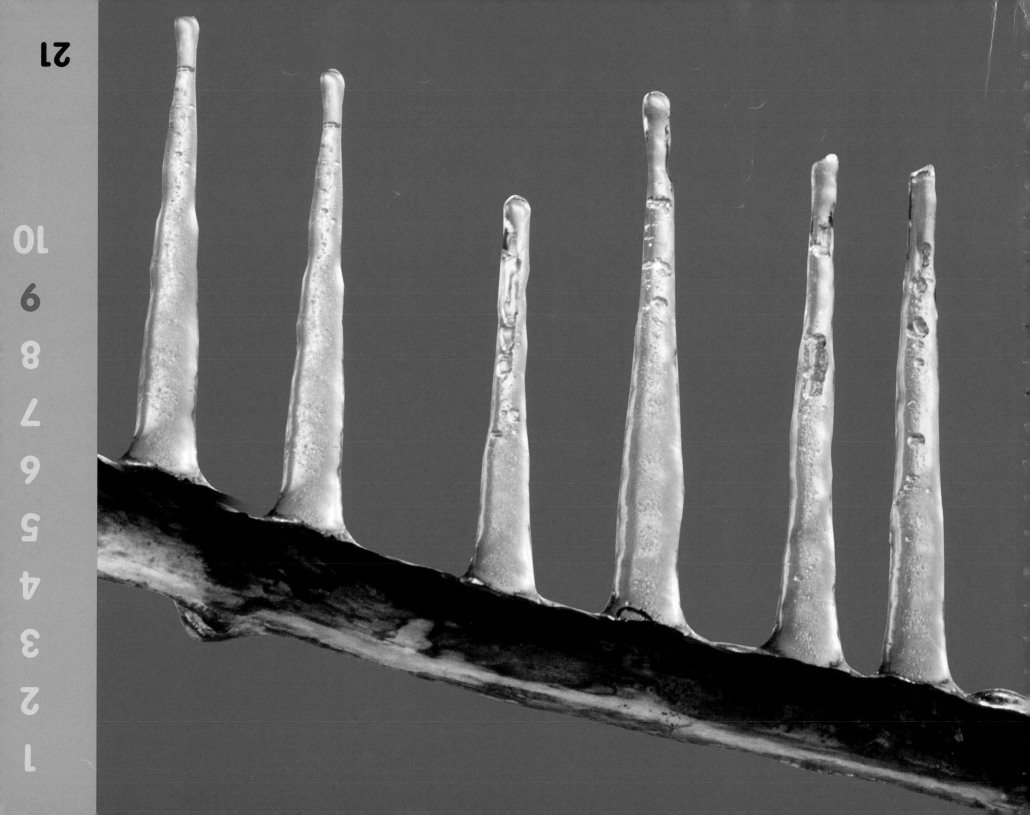

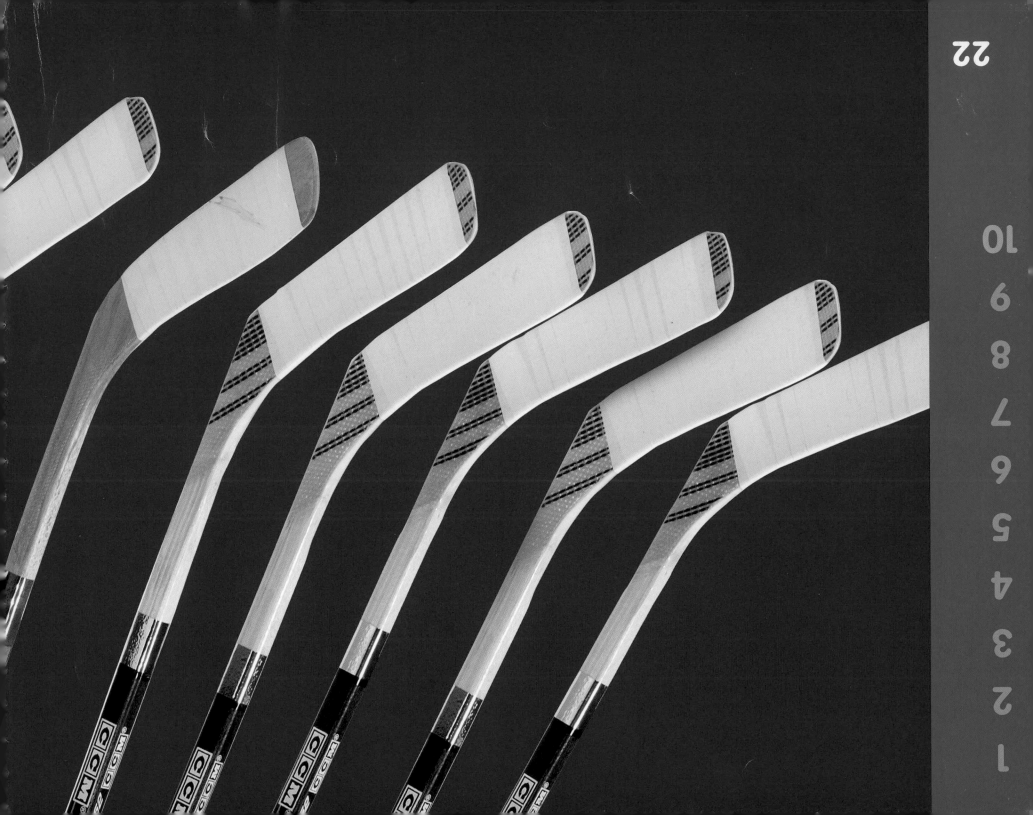

10

Ten sticks for hockey, who
wants to play? The game
is perfect on any wintry day.

Days are short and nights are longer. Temperatures are cold and the wind is stronger. It's fun to play on the ice and snow. Grab a snowball—ready, set, throw!

Sleds

Skaters

How Many?

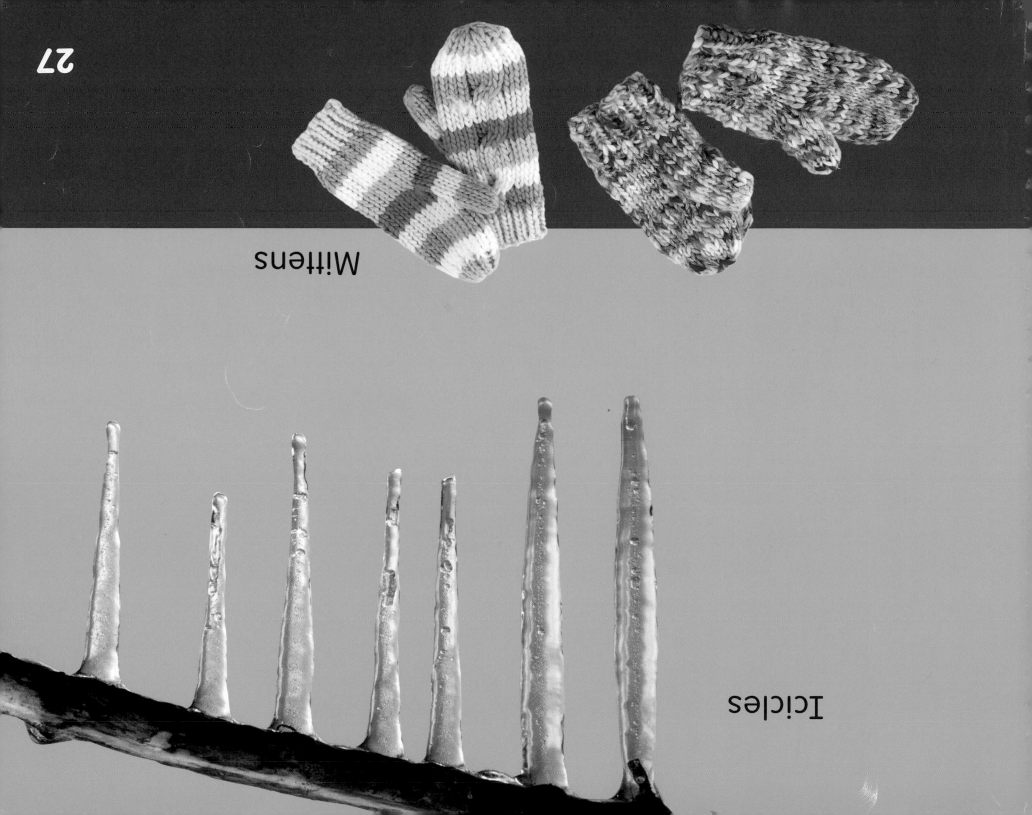

Mittens

Icicles

Facts about Winter

Cardinals are red birds with crests on their heads. Male cardinals have brighter feathers than females.

Every single snowflake has six sides. But no two snowflakes are exactly alike.

Huskies are the most common kind of sled dog. Huskies' thick fur keeps them warm in snow and cold temperatures. Sled dogs wear booties to protect their feet from sharp ice.

Icicles are formed when snow starts to melt. When snow melts on a roof or tree branch, it turns into water and drips off the edge. If this water freezes again while it drips, icicles form.